HOW TO START A REVOLUTION

Lucy-Anne Holmes founded the No More Page 3 campaign in 2012. She is also an actress and writer. She has written four novels – *50 Ways to Find a Lover*, *The (Im)Perfect Girlfriend*, *(Un)like a Virgin* and most recently *Just a Girl, Standing in Front of a Boy*, which is nominated for the Best Romantic Comedy Novel at the Romantic Novelists Awards.

HOW TO START A
REVOLUTION

LUCY-ANNE HOLMES

CORGI BOOKS

TRANSWORLD PUBLISHERS
61–63 Uxbridge Road, London W5 5SA
www.transworldbooks.co.uk

Transworld is part of the Penguin Random House group of companies
whose addresses can be found at global.penguinrandomhouse.com

Penguin
Random House
UK

First published in Great Britain in 2015 by Corgi Books and Transworld
Digital, imprints of Transworld Publishers

A CIP catalogue record for this book
is available from the British Library.

ISBN
9780552172066

Typeset in 9.3/13pt Palatino by Falcon Oast Graphic Art Ltd.
Printed and bound by Clays Ltd, Bungay, Suffolk.

Penguin Random House is committed to a sustainable
future for our business, our readers and our planet. This book is made
from Forest Stewardship Council® certified paper.

MIX
Paper from
responsible sources
FSC® C018179
www.fsc.org

1 3 5 7 9 10 8 6 4 2

For HQ

'I said, "Somebody should do something about that."
Then I realized I am somebody.'

Lily Tomlin

'Whatever you can do, or dream you can, begin it.
Boldness has genius, power and magic in it.'

Goethe

Introduction

I started an online petition.

That online petition turned into a campaign.

The campaign became a movement.

And, it's widely believed, that movement caused the most powerful 'family' (their word) newspaper in Britain to stop showing pictures of topless or naked young women on its third page. Something it had been doing for forty-five years and claimed was a 'British institution'.

I'd never campaigned on anything before. I am not particularly political or media savvy. Blimey, I'm not even confrontational. If someone bumps into me I say sorry. And I'm hopeless on a computer.

So if I can start a movement, anyone can. This book tells the story of how No More Page 3 began, but I've popped in a few pointers just in case you fancy starting a revolution yourself – something I thoroughly recommend.

How my
revolution started

You only need one thing to start a campaign and it isn't cash, experience, a thick skin or the ability to use Wordpress. It's passion. If you have enough of it you'll find that everything else will somehow be all right. It will be passion that will give you the bravery to stand up and start speaking out in the first place, and it will be passion that will keep you going despite insults and death threats and the fact that two years have gone by and the people you're appealing to are responding in frankly gobsmacking ways.

In my experience, passion doesn't always pop up and accost you with a raging fervour. Passion can start in a much gentler way.

My own passion started with a sense of unease; a feeling of being weirded out. When this feeling refused to go away, I began to look deeper, to try to find out what was going on.

It all started in the Olympic summer of 2012. I got embarrassingly excited by the London Olympics. I bought new trainers; I thought about setting up a five-a-side football team – I didn't do it, but I thought about it. I was inspired. And the thing that inspired me was the example of the women who trained so hard, competed and then stood there triumphant and tearful on the medal podiums. It was a great time for women in sport, and for once female athletes got a look-in on the sports pages.

Usually, press coverage of sport is male-dominated. Women get just 5 per cent of column inches in the sports sections of Britain's newspapers. The Olympics was a rare exception to this rule, and I made the most of it. I wanted to learn all I could about these heroines.

The *Sun* was in my household while I was growing up. My brother always reckoned it was the best newspaper for sport, so when Jessica Ennis won her terrific gold medal for the heptathlon, I bought a copy of the *Sun* hoping to read all about it.

When I opened the paper, I didn't see a topless image on page 3, and I checked on page 5 and there wasn't one there either. I assumed the *Sun* had dropped the feature while the Olympics was on.

I was on the train, reading about Team GB, when I turned to page 13 and saw a massive image of a beautiful young woman in her knickers. It was strange. I'd grown up with these images in the paper, but on that day when I saw it, it suddenly felt as though I'd been slapped in the face and told it was a man's world. This was the largest female image, larger by far than the photos of Jessica Ennis winning gold for Britain, larger than any photo of any other woman in the whole paper. The dominant image of a woman in the *Sun* that day was a young woman showing her breasts for men. Yet this was a family newspaper. I couldn't help but wonder what it was saying about a woman's place in society.

Start your revolution

- What are the issues you feel passionately about? Either by yourself or with friends, brainstorm the questions: 'What really pisses me off?' and 'What do I want to change in society?'
- Don't try to be tactical or guess what cause people are likely to get behind. Find something YOU wholeheartedly believe in – and most likely others will too.

Do your homework

I don't know whether you've ever experienced that chain reaction when one thought seems to open a door to another thought and then another and another. But this was what happened to me with Page 3. I got to the point where I could not stop thinking about it, even waking in the night with 'And another thing . . . !'

All sorts of ideas and questions were occurring to me about the display of pictures of naked women in family newspapers. What was it teaching little girls about where their value might lie? What was it teaching little boys about how to respect women?

I thought back to my friends with children and their accounts of being asked to move on or being made to feel uncomfortable over breastfeeding in public.

I replayed in my mind the most common expressions I'd heard in response to these pictures: 'Cor, look at the tits on that!' or 'I'd do/bang/ruin that!' And for the first time it occurred to me that 'she' and 'her' had given way to 'that'. Something about the context of these images meant that the women in them turned into a 'that'. An object. They were being dehumanized. And yet we know throughout history that when we allow people to be dehumanized some pretty bad stuff can happen to them.

This got me thinking about some of the bad stuff that happens to women. I looked up sexual assault and rape statistics. I found a report that said that 1 in 4 women will experience sexual assault in their lifetime. My first reaction was disbelief: surely the figure couldn't be that high? But I had personal experience that said otherwise. In my early twenties, I was sexually assaulted. I didn't report it, I told no one – except a female friend. And when I confided in her, she told me she'd been raped, yet she had hardly told anyone either. So I started asking women about their experiences, and the results were horrifying. They weren't just telling me about one incident but two, three or four. And the more accounts of sexual violence against women that I heard, the more I asked myself: if this is as serious an issue as I'm learning, is it sensible to be showing women naked in a family newspaper?

I also began to think about the impact Page 3 has on women's self-esteem and body image. I realized that I had been ashamed of my breasts since they arrived when I was eleven. When men in the society around you are commenting on the breasts on Page 3, you absorb the fact that breasts are a pretty big deal, that as a woman your breasts are there for men to look at and it's important that they look like the ones in the paper.

No matter which way I looked at it, I couldn't see that these pictures were doing women any favours.

My goal wasn't to get naked pictures of women

banned; what I wanted was for women to be respected in the media, the way men are.

So I spent a long time honing a letter to the editor of the *Sun* asking him to stop showing the topless pictures. 'I'll bullet point my reasons, because there are quite a few . . .' I began, and went on for three pages. Even as I posted it, I knew it wouldn't achieve anything. Yet I still had this passion for my cause; it wasn't going away. In fact, it was growing. And I wondered, if it could generate all this passion in me, maybe it would do the same in others. Could it be that I wasn't the only one who felt this way?

I soon found other people who shared the same views and they joined me on the campaign.

Start your revolution

- Think, think and think some more about your issue and why you want to see change.
- What are your arguments? Can you find evidence to support them? Break them all down to make a big list.
- Has anyone campaigned on this in the past? Or are they campaigning now? You might prefer to add value to their campaign with your support or you may feel that there is space for you to start something yourself. Whatever you decide, send them an 'in solidarity' message and let them know your plans.

Name your cause

I love the name No More Page 3 but I admit that a name that starts with a 'no' can have a tendency to make people feel defensive. It can make them think you're out to take something away from them, deny them something they want. Would I have attracted more followers if I'd gone for a more positive ask and name? Maybe instead of saying no to breasts I should have said yes to . . . balls.

'Balls on Page 3' had the potential to be witty:

Dear Editor of the *Sun*,
Please can we see big, young, hairless scrotums on Page 3. Fair's fair!

I could definitely see the benefits of this.

- Scrotums and breasts both being globe-shaped, it could be a creative and interesting way to request equal representation (a topless man wouldn't have been equal in the same way).
- I could dismiss any opposition with the lines that were constantly directed at me: 'Oh, you're only jealous because yours aren't up to much' and

'Don't be such a killjoy, you prude. It's a bit of fun, that's all.'

I may be wrong, but I reckon a lot of people would have signed a petition for 'Balls on Page 3', even if it was only for the novelty value.

But there was one big problem with the 'Balls on Page 3' campaign, and that was that I didn't want to see balls on page 3. Nothing against the male scrotum, but having grown up in a society that holds women up to the impossible ideal of Page 3, the last thing I wanted was to incite something that would leave a generation of men feeling paranoid or ashamed about their scrotums. There is no way I could have spent two and a half years banging on about balls, and I'm sure that the unbelievable team I came to work with, who offered endless support and countless hours of graft as the campaign grew, wouldn't have got up at six in the morning before work to write blogs, to respond to supporters, to tend to our social media channels, purely in the hope of seeing young men's testicles on the pages of a family newspaper.

The reason I plumped for No More Page 3 as a name was because it met all the criteria:

- It did what it said on the tin, summing up what the campaign was about.
- It was short and punchy.

- It wasn't already in use.
- It didn't form an unfortunate acronym like F.A.I.L.

A name needs to be fairly short or capable of being shortened effectively so that it can function as a Twitter name and website URL. People might mistype a long and complicated name such as www.letsridtheworld ofnucleararms.com – and if that happens, chances are they won't bother to make a second attempt.

Once you've come up with a name, check that someone else isn't using it already. You'd be gutted if you paid out for flyers and T-shirts to promote your website campaigning for more women in leadership positions, only to find that the domain name www.womenontop. com had already been taken – and the website in question had a very different interpretation of 'women on top' to the one you were trying to get across.

Start your revolution

- Pinpoint your ask.
- Choose your name accordingly.
- It needs to reflect, as simply and pithily as possible, whatever it is you want to achieve.
- Do a web search to check it isn't already in use.
- While you're online, think about buying the domain name. Just type 'buy a domain name' and Google will take you through it.

Pick your target

Chances are there will be people in a position to give you what you want.

In my case those individuals were:

- The editor of the *Sun* newspaper.
- Rupert Murdoch, the owner of the paper.
- David Cameron, Prime Minister at the time of the campaign.

I opted to direct my appeal for No More Page 3 to the editor of the paper, making the decision by a process of elimination.

Rupert Murdoch, the eighty-odd-year-old billionaire media mogul who owns the newspaper, was based in the USA and Australia. I didn't have an address for him and even though ultimately he could make the decision, he seemed a bit spectre-like and too far removed to be a target.

There were a host of reasons why I didn't want to ask David Cameron. For a start, this wasn't a campaign to make it illegal to show breasts in the press. After all, there could be a time in the future where we all get together and say, 'Let's celebrate the fact we're incredible, sensual, sexual, beautiful beings by capturing this in a photograph that makes everyone, regardless of gender, age, race or sexual orientation feel completely included!' I didn't fancy the prospect of this plan being scuppered by an editor saying, 'Sorry, we'll have to pixelate the nipples because Lucy-Anne Holmes got them banned in 2012.'

Besides, I felt a complete lack of connection to our Prime Minister – and not just him but the coalition government, the cabinet, and the other main party leaders at the time. I found politics bewildering. I'd sit squinting at the radio during the Prime Minister's Questions broadcast. A bunch of posh men baying at, and blaming, each other didn't seem to me the most mature or sensible way to govern a nation. Or I'd watch the news and see politicians, the majority of them male, slagging each other off and avoiding answering questions.

That left the editor of the *Sun*. He was responsible for the content of the newspaper, and the *Sun*'s offices were in London. Perfect.

There have been two *Sun* editors in the time I've been campaigning: Dominic Mohan when I started out, and David Dinsmore at the time of writing. I don't think either of them were that keen on me. Especially when it became apparent that, fuelled by passion for the cause, the No More Page 3 campaign was stronger in its convictions than the *Sun*.

The *Sun* was motivated by sales and profit. It was the job of the editor to support Page 3 whatever his personal views might be.

When asked, 'Why do you want Page 3 to go?' the NMP3 campaign supporters could come up with a wealth of heartfelt reasons, along with first-hand testimony as to how we had been affected by it. As a result, we moved people and brought them along with us. When asked, during the course of the Leveson Inquiry, why Page 3 was there, *Sun* editor Dominic Mohan replied, 'I mean, this was first published 42 years ago, erm, and I think it's meant to represent the youth and freshness and it celebrates natural beauty.'

I always felt that the editors couldn't carry on indefinitely trying to justify the unjustifiable and all we had to do was keep challenging them.

When you pitch passion against profit, I believe passion will come out the winner. But be warned – it may take a while.

Start your revolution

- Determine who has the power to grant your request.
- Find out how to contact them direct.
- Bear in mind that they are likely to ignore you to begin with. Be prepared for the long haul.

Start a petition

So you've decided what you want to say and to whom
. . . now it's time to make yourself heard.

Your little voice will struggle to make an impression
all by itself. But there are people out there who share
your views and who will join their voices to yours.
Once that happens, all this sense you're talking will
become so deafening that the powers that be will have
no choice but to sit up and take notice. Maybe even
capitulate.

But how do you get other voices to join your own?
What's the best way to create a platform so that others
can join you?

The good news is, it's never been easier. Thanks to
Tim Berners-Lee and his unbelievably kind gift of the
Internet, we now have at our fingertips the means to
form communities and effect change.

The platform I chose was the online petition, and
I thoroughly recommend it. People will scoff 'click-
tivism, slacktivism', but face it: whatever you do,
people will scoff – so let them. Although I have to warn
you, if you're liking the sound of a bit of slacktivism,
you should know that there is nothing slack about
online campaigning. On the contrary: it's exciting,

manic, relentless. Oh, and it doesn't do sleep.

It probably comes as no surprise that I am a massive fan of the online petition. You don't have to make it the be-all and end-all, but as a sort of heart that beats at the centre of your campaign, it's invaluable.

When Iain Duncan Smith, the government's Work and Pensions Secretary, stated on BBC Radio 4's *Today* programme that he could live on £7.57 a day, or £53 a week, Dom Aversano launched a petition on Change.org challenging him to 'Prove it IDS'. Over 400,000 people have signed that petition, and as a result all the major news programmes covered the story, highlighting the issues of benefits cuts and how the majority of the population felt that politicians were out of touch.

Online petitions are a brilliant resource because:

- Every time someone signs your online petition an email is sent to the person you are appealing to.*
- You can email everyone who has signed the petition, keeping them updated with your campaign's developments and asking them to help.*
- People provide their reasons for signing. Not only does this allow you to hear the many voices speaking out with you, it can provide slogans for your cause. For many, the NMP3 campaign's tagline became 'news not boobs'; this was coined by a supporter on the petition page.*

- The online petition sites are impartial, but they can offer really valuable advice on things from press releases to death threats.*
- The petition gives you a visible tally, allowing you to monitor your progress and whoop about how mighty you're getting.

I chose Change.org to host my petition, and I'm so glad I did. I found them by Googling 'best online petition sites'. Among the search results was an article that listed five sites and gave reasons why they were the pick of the bunch. I decided on Change.org because the site looked clean and easy to use.

The only site I would not use is the government site that creates e-petitions. Many have been tempted to do this because of the statement on the site's 'how-it-works' page: 'If you collect 100,000 signatures, your e-petition could be debated in the House of Commons'. Note the crucial word 'could'. Don't be fooled into false optimism. For 'could be debated', read 'practically guaranteed not to be debated'. The problem seems to be that they suffer 'death by committee', with a lot of petitions going over the 100,000 signature mark and yet still not leading to a debate.

If you are my mum, you will be tutting as you read

---

* Not true for e-petitions.direct.gov.uk, the government's official online petition website.

this and saying, 'I've never signed an online petition in my life! Come on, Lucy, I've only sent that one text message. What about me?'

While I wholeheartedly believe that the Internet is a lush and fertile ground for effective campaigning tools, if you were to ask me, 'Could NMP3 have done it without the Internet?' the answer would be yes. Of course it would be yes. The suffragettes did it without mobile phones. With passion you can do anything, remember!

It would be a very different proposition though. For a start you'd need cash to pay for phone calls, paper, printing, etc. If your budget could run to paying for advertising, that would be even better. You'd have to get out on the street to kick things off, ideally with some headline-grabbing stunt (maybe the suffragettes can give you some inspiration), collecting signatures, engaging with people. You may well still get there in the end, but it could take a long time. Bear in mind, it took us two and a half years – and that was with the Internet.

Start your revolution

- Start a petition, online or otherwise. It's free and easy to do.

Get brainstorming

Gah, it seemed I'd started a campaign! Unsure of what on earth I was supposed to do next, and lacking any campaigning knowledge or experience, I got out a pen and a piece of paper and started making a list.

I wrote down all the things that I could feasibly do to help this campaign I seemed to have launched:

- Write stuff – blogs and articles – about Page 3 and how it affected me.
- Ask creative friends to lend a hand and contribute something for the campaign.
- Contact writers/actors and ask them to come up with comedy sketches to get the message across?
- Ask musicians/songwriters to write a campaign song?
- Film myself talking about the issues and put it on YouTube/blog.
- Logo . . .

I got quite flummoxed by the last item on that list. I didn't know anyone who did graphic design, but it seemed to me that a logo was an important thing to have. My friend's ex-husband had a T-shirt making business, and I thought it would be great advertising if I could print No More Page 3 on a T-shirt and photograph someone in it. I didn't know any more about T-shirt design than I did logos, but I recalled that when I was growing up the band Frankie Goes to Hollywood had T-shirts with FRANKIE SAYS RELAX in big clear black writing. I decided to write No More Page 3 in the same way. To start with I ordered a hundred T-shirts, thinking I could sell them and donate the money to my sister-in-law's breast cancer charity.

They were a huge hit from the start, with people queuing up to buy them. The T-shirts became a wonderfully effective way to spread the message. I sometimes think that the No More Page 3 T-shirt will turn out to have been one of the best ideas I ever had. One of my favourite pictures from the campaign is of Caroline Lucas, MP for Brighton Pavilion, during Prime Minister's Questions. She is sitting up, alert in her NMP3 T-shirt, surrounded by people, mostly men, in dark suits, some of whom look to be asleep.

Start your revolution

- Brainstorm your campaign. Write down any thought that comes into your mind, no matter how random. Some you will end up discarding, but you might come across some gems along the way.

- Ask yourself 'If money, time, etc was no object . . . what would I do?'
- Then ask 'What can I feasibly do?'
- Brainstorm 'Who might be able to help me?' List famous/influential people you could target along with any friends or family who come into your mind.

Speak from the heart

As you set about writing bits and bobs, such as the blurb for your petition, blog entries and letters for the campaign, you may be wondering how this public voice of yours should sound.

In the early days of the campaign an article in the *Guardian* reported: '*Sun* editor is asked, sweetly and politely, to drop Page 3.'

Sweetly and politely – not the most badass campaigning credentials.

Some people said I should have been bolder and angrier, but that's just not me. I went to a Catholic school where 'blessed are the meek' was drummed into us. It came as a bit of a shock to the family when I stood up against the *Sun* on the subject of boobs.

So I just asked as me. Many people commented that they loved the tone of the campaign, which was interesting because we were just using our own voices. Perhaps it goes to show that people soon cotton on when organizations or individuals speak to us with voices that aren't authentic.

I say 'oooo' and 'lovely' a lot, and both words often cropped up in our bulletins. The aim was always to bring people into the debate rather than to lecture them or tell them what they should think. We wanted a platform that was warm and welcoming rather than formal, intimidating or angry. For myself, and many of the NMP3 team and supporters, Page 3 had flicked a switch, making us interested in feminism, politics and activism. We were aware that it was the same for many of those who found us online, and it was important to us that No More Page 3 was a welcoming place.

Start your revolution

- Be yourself. Use your own voice in your campaign. It sometimes feels like everyone is speaking bollocks to get our votes or our cash. Let's try to speak from the heart and not add to the bollocks.
- If possible, be real, be warm – and get your funny out.

Social media

The time had come to start spreading the word, and that's where social media comes into its own.

Twitter

Far and away the most effective means of spreading the word about No More Page 3, especially in the early days, was via Twitter.

I wasn't a fan of Twitter back then. I'd gone on it very reluctantly when my publishers insisted that I start tweeting to help promote a book I'd written. 'I don't want to tell people what I had for breakfast,' I moaned. I didn't get Twitter. It seemed so frenetic and 140 characters didn't seem nearly enough to say anything of value.

It was my nineteen-year-old niece Kathryn who insisted we get a Twitter account for No More Page 3. Within minutes I was hooked. Within an hour I was in some frenzied tweeting paroxysm.

Twitter is incredible for launching a campaign. You can reach anyone! You can tweet David Cameron, Stephen Fry, Caitlin Moran. Everyone! Even though they probably won't respond, there is always a slim chance that they might, so it is worth a pop! We set about tweeting the link to the petition to . . . um, well, everyone.

The only slight downside to this is that, if you send too many unsolicited tweets, Twitter thinks you're spamming people and you get suspended. But we were always quickly reinstated.

Thanks to our efforts, one journalist wrote that the No More Page 3 campaign would be coming soon 'to a Twitter feed near you'.

'Hello, new followers. Welcome to the revolution!' We'd whoop as the total of our followers went up and up. Oh and we'd whoop about the signatures on the petition going up too. There was a lot of whooping. Very often with an @nomorepage3 Whooop! We are doing this! Then we started BOOMing. We loved a BOOM. We did a countdown for every thousand names we amassed on the petition until the end. Counting down with

> @nomorepage3 4!! Just 4 more of your finest
> signatures needed and we will be a community
> of 30,000 people!!! We are doing this!!!

I dread to think how many exclamation marks we used in the entire campaign – I blame the passion.

Essentially we built a campaign through Twitter, and it was a terrific platform for showing that No More Page 3 was warm, alive and meant business. Someone could learn about the campaign, find our Twitter feed and see that we were there, speaking out, serious about seeing the end of Page 3, whether it be a Sunday morning or late on a Tuesday evening.

Facebook

Facebook was a totally different beast. It was a much, much slower burn to create a community on Facebook than with Twitter. But it turned out to be worth the slow cooking, because the Facebook community that was nurtured became mighty and glorious. More signatures were added to our petition via Facebook than any other source.

You see, with Twitter you send a tweet, it lands in people's feeds, but those feeds are always moving, always busy. Content hangs around for longer in Facebook feeds and pages, which means there's a greater chance it will be read, seen or shared widely.

Plus you don't have the infuriating 140-character limitation. On Facebook supporters have space to debate, and it's because of this space that a real community forms. We know that many of our supporter groups came together as a result of acquaintances and friendships formed on the No More Page 3 Facebook page.

Unfortunately there were the occasional visits from people who thought it would be nice to post porn on our page or pop up to tell us to f*** off, so the Facebook page did need a bit of policing.

We shared content daily on Facebook, as we did on Twitter too; mainly articles directly related to Page 3 or media sexism, or pictures of supporters in T-shirts – whether they were on stage, up Ben Nevis, on someone's shoulders at a festival, holding their baby . . . We were sent an endless stream of pictures of supporters in No More Page 3 T-shirts, as well as various creative protests, such as 'No More Page 3' written in chalk on pavements, on sand on beaches, in snow, with pastry on pies, icing on cupcakes, on bunting or Christmas decorations.

People found a host of ways to explore the issue using their talents, so it wasn't just photos we shared but creative content including a variety of songs (choral, rap, folk, gospel), poems, plays and short films.

Naturally we did a lot of whooping about this wonderful shareable content that flowed all the way through the campaign. Saying thank you and expressing our gratitude to supporters was something we did a lot. We were well aware that it wasn't always easy for people to express their support. One supporter told me she hadn't spoken to her brother for three months because he disagreed with her support for the campaign. A number of us in the team had had disagreements with people we loved over No More Page 3, so we could identify with the problems our supporters faced. As a result we were genuinely grateful for every share on social media, for all the occasions when someone wore their T-shirt, for every time someone stepped out of their comfort zone and spoke up about the campaign. It took a lot of bravery, and we never lost sight of that.

Blog

'Words, Lucy, you need words!'

That was the message from John Coventry, at Change.org, when I was starting out. 'Your argument is powerful so make it strongly and clearly as often as possible in as many places as possible. Blogs, comment pieces, interviews. Set the debate on your terms, as early as possible.'

John Coventry knows what he's talking about. We tried to keep up the momentum, churning out words wherever we could, in blogs, posts and on videos, conveying the message from different angles and viewpoints. It will get to the point where it's not all coming from you and the people who form your team, but in the early days you can expect to do a fair bit of it.

And it's no use having great information, thoughts and ideas in your head – they need to be written down, so they can be shared. It's no good having sixty MPs who support you if it's not recorded somewhere so that people can see or share it. This sort of information will fuel your campaign – but the only way it will ever get out there is if you speak publicly. So get as many words down as you can about your campaign.

Setting up a free, easy-to-use blog for your campaign will start you off nicely. There you can make available all the information about your venture, with links for supporters, and blog posts, detailing your arguments and suggesting what action might be taken.

I think one of the cleverest and simplest ways we used our blog was with our Politicians' Letter. It became such a powerful document of support, and yet all we did was write a short letter addressed to the editor of the *Sun* and post it on the blog as a template:

Dear Dominic Mohan,
We write to lend our support to the No More
Page 3 campaign. As politicians our role is
to serve the people, and we cannot remain
silent in the presence of a page that limits and
misrepresents over half the population . . .

MPs should really only respond to requests by their own constituents, so we asked and encouraged supporters to email or tweet their MPs, urging them to add their names to the letter. We helped supporters out by offering sample letters, which they could send to their MPs, and resources so they could find their contact details.

As a result, we amassed support from over 160

cross-party MPs (only a handful of whom were Conservatives), a host of MSPs, Members of the Welsh Assembly, MEPs and councillors. Some of these politicians didn't just add their names to the campaign, they also wrote blogs of support or offered us assistance in other ways.

Start your revolution

- Choose your social media weapons of choice and start spreading the word.
- We focused on the powerful combination of online petition, Twitter, Facebook and blog to get the message out about No More Page 3. There are a host of other online platforms that might also appeal to you, including Instagram, Tumblr and YouTube.
- Set up a free and easy-to-use blog or site and begin to amass as much information about your cause as possible there.
- Start getting your words and arguments down in blog posts on your own site and asking other allies to do the same either on their own blogs or as guest blog posts on yours.

The power
of the press

Even better than a blog about your campaign is an article in a newspaper about your campaign. Ideally, this would be a supportive article, but as someone who has had a fair few unsupportive articles I can tell you that they too can prove useful. In fact one of the things that really got the campaign under way was a particularly scathing article. Other commentators immediately leapt to my defence, so thanks to that one negative write-up I got three positive articles written in response.

That's not to say it didn't feel ghastly at the time. Reading an attack on you and the campaign you've started isn't something you want to do regularly. Mind you, when Brendan O'Neil in the *Telegraph* moaned, 'Is there no end to the feminist nagging about Page 3?' it made me chuckle: 'Ha, we haven't even started yet, Brendan!'

So don't worry too much about negative press. I say that because, if you're anything like I was, it's bound to get to you a bit. Before the campaign I had a mistrust of the press. The goings-on exposed by the Leveson Inquiry had me terrified that the press would misquote me or, worse still, make something up about me. I definitely didn't imagine that the press could be sympathetic or on my side in any way. I was so nervous before my first interview, which came a few weeks into the campaign off the back of a press release, I locked myself in a room beforehand to have a good cry.

I needn't have worried. The article was terrific; the journalist not only quoted me verbatim, they picked out the best bits and ignored all the waffley stuff. The words and picture took up nearly two pages in the G2 section of the *Guardian* (spanning Page 3). It made the campaign sound exciting. We were off. The signatures on the e-petition rocketed on the strength of just that one article.

In fact, every journalist I spoke to throughout the course of the campaign was brilliant. I don't think I was misquoted or misconstrued once. If I did mistrust a particular journalist, as I admit I did when we had a request from the *Daily Mail* – my mum reads it and quite often remarks when they have to apologize for making things up – I simply asked to do the interview via email. That way I would have proof of exactly what I'd told them, should I need it.

Start your revolution

It's time to tell the press about your campaign:

- Write a press release.

    Don't be scared by the term 'press release'. It's just a couple of paragraphs of basic information about whatever you want the press to know. Make sure you include details of your social media pages, blog URL and a name and contact number should readers require more information.
- Create/get your hands on a press list.

    To start with you can get press addresses from newspaper websites online. But I would also recommend asking your contacts and any sympathetic allies if they can supply you with relevant press lists. I found that people were very generous about sharing resources.
- Send out your press release.
- Prepare yourself for calls/emails from journalists. What points would you like to get across in an interview?

Dealing with abuse

Now that the press are on board your message begins to spread beyond your existing circles of friends and family and colleagues. People come to you, wanting to sign your petition and pledge support. But as you widen your net you'll catch some nasties too. Trolls will appear from the recesses of the Internet to call you a c***, to tell you to die, to say that you should 'f*** off' because you've got 'shit tits'. Or, my absolute favourite: that you should 'get a life'.

If – no, sorry, *when* – you start your campaign you will realize that speaking up passionately for what you believe in is one of the most incredible experiences you can have. You will discover skills you didn't realize you had, you'll find yourself embarking on adventures and meeting incredible people. You will certainly feel as though you have got a life. Far more of a life, I would hazard a guess, than someone who writes insults, abuse or threats to people online, often hiding behind a cloak of anonymity.

The threats and abuse that people – and in particular women who speak up about matters of inequality – face on the Internet has been widely documented. Sadly, it's all too common.

There are a variety of ways of dealing with it:

Ignore

For the most part, this was my preferred method, especially in the early days before the terrific NMP3 HQ team was formed and I had the virtual support of wonderful people at all times. When I was starting out, I just didn't have the energy to deal with the abuse. I went through a period where I would try to respond to everyone, even if it meant sitting up past midnight trying to debate or reason with a seventeen-year-old who was operating on so many levels of disrespect that it was difficult to get my head around it. I found it draining at best and depressing at worst. I realized that I didn't have limitless energy and I would rather use what reserves I had to stoke the positivity of the campaign rather than dwell on the negativity. And there was always far, far more positivity. The negative stuff made up a fraction of the feedback we received.

Report

Even if you are going to ignore it, you should consider blocking and reporting the perpetrator. In fact, before you really get going with your social media channels, I suggest you have a pootle around the various sites and check out how to report abuse. It's possible that by the time you actually come to reporting your first threatening or abusive tweet you may be shaken and so upset by it that negotiating the site's complaints procedure is the last thing you feel capable of doing.

And do consider contacting the police. The Crown Prosecution Service states that offensive content via social media is criminal when it involves:

- Credible threats (to a person's life or safety or property).
- Communications targeting specific individuals (including persistent harassment and ongoing abuse).
- Breach of court orders (for example, identifying people protected by law).
- Communications which are grossly offensive, indecent, obscene or false.

Google your local police force, and search 'offensive messages and posts on social media' for specific details of how to file a report.

Draw attention to it

Some people shame the abusers by drawing attention to the offending post. You can do this on Twitter quite easily by retweeting (making public to your followers what he/she said) and/or responding. I once engaged with someone who wanted me dead; by the end of the Twitter conversation he had deleted the tweet and was agreeing that it's not the greatest thing to be saying to people. Often when you retweet a tweet of that nature other people will start to engage with the person who sent it; and it can happen that the perpetrator will either retreat or delete the tweet.

Start your revolution

- Always be guided by how you are feeling when it comes to dealing with trolls, naysayers and the not-so-nice. If you haven't got it in you to respond, then don't. Think about your energy levels and mental health when it comes to this area of campaigning.
- Seek advice, support or go to the police if necessary.

It takes a team

I've touched on the fact that campaigning can leave you feeling knackered and on the fact that this campaign wasn't about me, it was about 'we'. But let's elaborate on that. Aside from being exhausting, there's a danger you'll find yourself so immersed in your campaigning life that you will neglect the basics – like making sure you get adequate rest and proper meals, and allowing yourself those little rituals that keep you calm and stable, whether it be meditation or yoga sessions, or nights in onesies watching American serialized dramas.

Campaigning is wonderful and exhilarating, but it's manic. Putting something of yourself, something that you've created, out in the public sphere is draining in itself. On top of this you've got the pressure of speaking out about a controversial issue; dealing with your family and friends' responses; the impact of people disagreeing, patronizing, insulting and even threatening you. Then there's the stress of dealing with the press for the first time, whether it be print, radio or, scariest of all, the telly. As if that isn't enough, factor in the added workload that you will suddenly have, trying to make sure your social media channels are lively and informative, that you have enough content to share and there is enough for your supporters to get their teeth into.

Somehow, in the midst of all that, you need to think tactically. I remember once at a family dinner my father advising me, 'Lucy, look at it more as a marathon than a sprint.' I didn't really pay attention at the time – I was too busy sprinting to keep up with my Twitter feed. But he was so right.

There are many delicious goings-on as the campaign builds momentum: the highs feel incredible – you're wired with excitement, the adrenalin is surging as you teeter on the very edge of your comfort zone. In the whole grand scheme of your life, it's a wonderful place to be, but it can create tension in your mind and body. And if you're not looking after yourself, you may well burn out – which is what happened to me.

Burnout hit me like an overwhelming feeling of helplessness. I didn't know what was going on and it was terrifying. My shoulders were up around my ears. I was spent: financially, emotionally, creatively. I just didn't have any oomph left. And I hadn't a clue what to do about it. You can't campaign when you're like this, and yet the thing about campaigning is there is always a lot to do. Just going on Twitter with all those voices coming at me would bring on a panic attack. I felt as if I was being strangled by invisible hands. My thought processes got very dark. I remember thinking one morning: The only way to stop this feeling of so much to do and helplessness is to kill myself.

I didn't want to talk to anyone at the time. But one day another campaigner, Francine Hoenderkamp, Skyped me right after I'd turned my computer on, catching me off guard. She's so lovely and funny is Fran, I ended up explaining a bit about how I was feeling.

'Activists burn out, Luce,' she said. 'We all get it. We all fear it. You're all right. I've got your back.'

Just hearing that gave me a sense of relief. I took some time out to rest. And when I came back after a little break I realized that the campaign's demands on me hadn't changed – if anything there were more emails than ever to answer. But there had been a shift in my relationship to NMP3. I felt a bit stronger after my break, but I knew I couldn't go on trailblazing single-handedly.

It was possibly the darkest period of my life, but definitely of the campaign. And it was followed by what would turn out to be undoubtedly the most wonderful period.

I sent six emails to people I had got to know via our Facebook page or met at protests. I knew these people were as passionate as me, because they were ready to spend Saturday mornings in the bitter cold holding a placard, or whole evenings reasoning with people who came on our Facebook page to say, 'If you don't like it, don't buy it.' But most of all, I wrote to these people because I knew they were nice.

Nice. It's not a word we hear much about in all those 'We need to be beautiful, productive, rich' manuals and articles. But I sensed that these were kind, funny, down-to-earth people who I felt able to send an unsolicited message to, saying, 'Hello, I'm Lucy from No More Page 3, and I'm kind of fucked. Would you consider forming a team?'

They all came back with the kindest words and said YES (in capitals!) to starting a team.

It completely reenergized me and the campaign. Becoming a team, getting to know these glorious, talented, genius people and seeing them blow their energy on the campaign I'd started, well, it was incredible. Suddenly there was more womanpower to get stuff done, to create blog articles, and brainstorm ideas. We were a mighty team. It was so much fun. And really, if you're going to be giving up years of your life for a cause you believe in, you've got to enjoy it or it's just not sustainable.

Once, at a meeting, I asked them: 'How are we doing? Are we happy? Can we be doing this any better?' And my incredible teammate Stephanie Davies-Arai replied, 'I don't think I've ever been happier in my life.'

We were all on the edge of our comfort zones but growing so much. People said their confidence improved from the experience of campaigning, and they discovered they had skills they'd never suspected: writing, public speaking, debating, event organizing. For me the best part of the campaign was sharing it.

Start your revolution

- Ask yourself whether you need help.
- If the answer is yes, reach out. I found that people wanted to help, and generally enjoyed doing so. The highs you experience will be so much better when shared with a team, and when you face the lows there will be support, humour and a virtual or physical hug.

Forming alliances

The campaign taught me about the power of groups, both in terms of forming a team, and seeing all we could achieve as a collective, but also in the added strength we received when another big organization publicly lent us their support. A lone organization becomes far, far more powerful when supported by other organizations.

Almost seventy organizations and charities lent their voices to ours during the course of the campaign. Perhaps the most exciting of these alliances was with UK Girlguiding, whose young members had recently formed an advocacy arm. They stumbled across the campaign via social media and immediately embraced it, voting that No More Page 3 should be the first cause for the new advocacy group to get behind. They wrote a moving letter to the editor of the *Sun* (which he ignored), made a plea to David Cameron and accomplished a wave of mainstream press interviews. One young member even managed to engage in a totally calm and reasoned debate on the *Today* programme, the thought of which fills me with terror.

Our supporters put a huge amount of effort into persuading other organizations to join the campaign, forming their own No More Page 3 groups within their unions, universities or schools. Often this meant a weary process of lobbying and following formal procedures, which had to be endured before official approval was forthcoming.

The effect was cumulative: we'd be whooping about the National Union of Teachers backing us, and another supporter would pipe up, 'I'll see if I can get my union to weigh in too.' These organizations would show their support by flagging it up on their website, telling their members about the campaign and even, in the case of Unison and GMB, offering us a meeting space. We listed this mighty directory of allies on our handy blog.

Start your revolution

- Draw up a list of organizations, groups or charities that might support your campaign.
- Contact them. Give a friendly introduction to your mission, ask if they might be able to support your endeavours, and if so can they give you a short statement of support.

Money talks

Your campaign is finally gathering speed, your social media communities are expanding, you're amassing plenty of signatures on your petition, more and more big supporting organizations are coming on board, you're getting press coverage, remembering to eat and sleep, and thoroughly enjoying the experience of campaigning . . . but you have yet to achieve the goal you set out to achieve.

Understandably, you may be getting a little impatient. So what more can you do to make the decision makers sit up and listen?

Follow the money
Every big business with a dodgy moral compass exists because a lot of people give them cash. In the case of the *Sun*, this cash comes from the punters who buy the paper, the companies who advertise in it, and the shareholders who support it. We therefore made it part of our ongoing strategy to focus on these groups and try to persuade them to rethink their allegiance or join us in putting pressure on the *Sun*.

Warning: following the big money (i.e. corporations rather than individuals) can be dispiriting. You and your campaign are fuelled by passion and these businesses are fuelled by profit, so at times it can seem as if you're talking completely different languages. You make a heartfelt plea to Tesco or whoever, asking them to reconsider the thousands they spend on advertising in the *Sun*, or the way they display the *Sun* with its often inappropriate front pages in prominent position – at child height – in stores. And they reply in defence of their position (basically telling you that Tesco is great). At first, anyway. Two years later Tesco changed their policy on one of these issues and stopped displaying tabloids at children's height. Whoop!

So, expect to be persistent in this area. Don't be disillusioned by the corporate cold shoulder or standard PR-speak responses you and your supporters will receive. It's important to keep up the pressure.

Even if you don't feel you are getting anywhere, chances are conversations will be going on internally, as employees have to pen these responses and work out what to say. Why not fill their days with your issue?

Start your revolution

- Make a list of the key sources of revenue your opposition relies on. Consider targeting one, a few, or all of these.
- To avoid getting a cut-and-paste response, try to

engage them in a proper conversation by asking specific questions. At least that way you will learn where they stand on your particular issue.

Fun, stunts and direct action

You will no doubt get to a point, or many points, where you want to do some campaign stunting. Yes, an urge might well grab you, like it did us, and you'll suddenly find yourself dressed in seventies gear, singing No More Page 3 to the tune of 'YMCA', whilst doing a choreographed dance routine in the drizzle outside the *Sun* offices. We did this to celebrate 100,000 signatures on the petition. We also drove a massive cardboard cut-out of a LEGO Page 3 model (Leanne, 22, from Legoland) up the M4 to LEGO head offices and Legoland for a visit. We were following the money, as LEGO had been giving away free children's toys during half terms for two years in the *Sun*. There would be pictures of LEGO on the front page, drawing children towards it, and then they'd open up the paper to see soft porn. A supporter started his own Change.org petition appealing to LEGO to stop doing this, but LEGO seemed to be ignoring the protest. So we took Leanne to meet them.

Also, if you are anything like me, then after two and a half years of campaigning politely and peacefully on the same issue you may start seriously considering direct action as a more forceful way of getting your message across. Or you may have bypassed the polite bit and be well under way with this already. There's no denying it can be incredibly effective. UK Uncut exploded into our consciousness when seventy people waving placards staged a sit-in outside the Oxford Street Vodafone flagship store to draw attention to tax avoidance allegations against the company. A video of this quickly went viral.

Stunts and actions can be fun, and meeting other team members and supporters in real life (as opposed to Twitter or Facebook life) always gives your morale a boost. They are great for generating press coverage, putting pressure on the decision makers and reminding/informing the wider public of your campaign.

Start your revolution

- Have a glorious brainstorm about what stunts and/or direct action you might want to do for your campaign.
- Opt for the one on your list that excites you and is doable.
- Tell your supporters about it. Message everyone who's signed your petition and spread the word on social media. It's a good idea to set up a separate Facebook group for the event. Keep reminding

people in the build-up to the big day.
- Send out a press release. Schedule a photo-call, so the media can come along and take photographs.

Revolution
ground rules

At the time of writing it's been over a month since we were informed – by sources at the *Sun* and by other media – that the *Sun* had dropped Page 3. Three days later, in response to the amount of press coverage the story had received, they brought it back. However, it was just for one day. There has been no official statement from the *Sun* about the end of Page 3 but we have been told by numerous sources that they won't be showing the daily pictures of topless young women any more. So, in short, it seems we've won.

I am so glad that we achieved what we did, but if I'm honest what I loved most about No More Page 3 was *how* we did it. We asked nicely, with humour, *tenaciously* for two and a half years, creating and maintaining a platform where people could find their voice and share their stories about the impact of the *Sun*'s portrayal of women on their lives.

I've told you how my revolution started, but how you set about your revolution will be down to you. Whether as an individual or part of a team, know that you can trust your instincts. If something doesn't feel right, don't do it.

At the same time, bear in mind that you may not always have the right answers. Seek advice and help, especially from supporters you've come to admire. You don't have to take it, but it might just arm you with a bit of useful wisdom.

You can't solve a problem by employing the same thinking that created it. If your adversary doesn't speak the truth, don't take them on by spinning your own web of lies. If you're campaigning against discrimination targeting a particular group, don't discriminate against another to win your case. If you feel something is unjust or immoral, don't stoop to unjust or immoral tactics yourself.

Let's not have campaigns that are inauthentic or that show traits such as greed, dishonesty and disrespect, like so many of the organizations we'll be active against. Let's make a new world with our beautiful campaigning.

Wishing you a wonderful time with your activism ;)

Some things you can do to start your revolution

- Find something you passionately believe in and are prepared to dedicate the time and effort to.
- Research the subject, come up with facts to support your argument.
- Choose a name that's pithy and hasn't already been taken.
- Find out who has the power to grant your request and establish contact.
- Start an online petition.
- Brainstorm your campaign. Come up with things you could do in an ideal world, if you had the money or time, as well as what can be done using the resources you have. Draw up a list of people who could help.
- Be authentic: speak in your own voice.
- Use social media to get your message across.
- Write a press release and send it to all relevant publications.
- Look after yourself. Take time out. It won't all disappear if you don't post anything on Facebook for a few days. And that space you give yourself may quieten your brain so you can hear the answers and get the inspiration you need.
- Don't be afraid to ask for help. Burnout is inevitable if you try to do it all alone. People who share your passion will often be all too willing to lend a hand.

- Approach organizations that might share your concerns and lend their support to your campaign.
- Make a list of the key sources of revenue your opposition relies on. Contact them and try to persuade them to reconsider their allegiance.
- If you make a mistake, own up and apologize. We found that our supporters responded kindly. As someone once said, 'To err is human, to apologize on social media is divine.'
- Everyone has an opinion, the secret is not to take it personally or get defensive. Take a breath and ask yourself: 'Is there any truth in this? Can we learn from it?' We would sometimes contact our critics and ask if they had any suggestions as to how we could do things better. Most of the time they didn't, but sometimes they offered constructive criticism.

Acknowledgements

I would like to acknowledge and thank everybody who signed the petition, who followed us on social media, who wore the T-shirt, who debated with family, friends and strangers, in person and online. For those of you who created regional groups, lobbied politicians, unions, schools, universities, and for all the charities and organizations who joined their voices to ours. No More Page 3 was made up of all the passion, intellect, creativity, time, love and humour that you gave it. That was what made it mighty. The experience of the campaign is part of us all now and I so hope we feel prouder and stronger for it.

HQ, I don't really know where to begin in thanking you all for the experiences we have had and continue to have. The fact that I even got to meet such inspiring, brave, clever, hilarious, wonderful people is awesome enough, but that we worked together on such a beautiful and important project is an experience I am just so humbled by and grateful for. I know it will always be a highlight of my life.

Masses of thanks to the fantabulous people at Change.org, who work so hard and care so much about people like me (and you) having a voice in society: John Coventry, Brie Rogers Lowry, Katherine Sladden and Kajal Odedra. Oh my goodness, I am so pleased I rather randomly picked Change.org that day. It was wonderful to make change with Change.org.

Huge thanks go to my friends for bearing with me when I fell off the planet for two and a half years. And to my family. Me speaking up about No More Page 3 was a huge challenge for my incredibly close family. I am so happy that we got through the difficult bits and that our love was stronger than our differing views.

Thanks to my agent, Rowan Lawton, for being so lovely and charmingly diffusing any uncomfortable situation, and especially for bearing with me when I committed client nightmare by suggesting people boycott the major supermarkets.

Finally, there are plenty of big and excited thanks left for all the wonderful people at Transworld. In particular to Helen Gregory who approached me to do this book with the particularly badass title (which I love), was so passionate about the project and worked with me so closely on it. And to the wonders that are Andrea Henry, Anne O'Brien, Alice Murphy-Pyle, Ben Willis, Naomi Mantin and Leah Feltham who worked hard to bring this book to life.

Oooo the acknowledgements have turned into an essay. I guess you'd best be off now to start some revolutions. Please do keep in touch, I'd be happy to help if I can. @lucyanneholmes